OUTRAGEOUS
Crossword Puzzle and Word Game Book for Kids

Helene Hovanec

**Introduction
by Will Shortz**

ST. MARTIN'S GRIFFIN
NEW YORK

Introduction

What is the difference between a riddle and a vase?

Take a couple of seconds to think. (One thousand and one, one thousand and two . . .)

Give up?

A riddle is best when cracked!

You'll be cracking lots of riddles like this in this *Outrageous Crossword Puzzle and Word Game Book for Kids*. It's a big collection of original mind bogglers that will tickle your brain and your funnybone at the same time. Besides crosswords, you'll find word finds, crisscrosses, fractured phrases, frame-ups, cross-offs, and many other types of puzzles. Usually, solving the puzzzle will help you answer a final, wacky riddle.

Perhaps you have seen your parents solve the crosswords that I edit for *The New York Times*. The puzzles in this book require the same cleverness to solve—but were created especially with your age in mind. Now put on your thinking cap, and good luck!

—WILL SHORTZ

How To Solve
by Helene Hovanec

Every puzzle is a little game between you, the solver, and me, the puzzle maker. I've hidden something in each puzzle for you to find. Think of yourself as a detective who is collecting clues, one by one. When you find all of them, you've solved the case! In this book, the solution is often the answer to an outrageous riddle which will make you laugh or groan.

For crosswords: Read each clue, and, if you know the answer, write the word into the grid either going across or down. If you don't know the answer, just skip that clue and go on to another one. Most people start with 1 Across, but you can start with any clue. There's no right or wrong way to solve a crossword. After you've solved the puzzle, you might have to do something else to find the riddle answer. Sometimes you'll have to read the circled letters from left to right and top to bottom. At other times you'll have to place letters from numbered spaces into the same numbered blanks below the grid. Always be sure to match up the numbers in both places.

For word finds: Circle each word very carefully, because the letters that you *don't* use will be important. You'll have to place those letters into blank spaces to find the answer to the riddle. When you're searching for the unused letters to write into the blanks, go from left to right and top to bottom and be sure not to skip any letters.

For fill-ins: Think of this puzzle as a type of jigsaw. Each word in the list fits into just one space in the grid. Always start with a letter that is already written in the grid. Count the number of boxes in the word that contains that letter. For example, it could be a 5-letter word that starts with B. There will be one 5-letter word that starts with B in the list. Write that word into the grid and work from there.

If you're stuck on a puzzle and can't go any further, just stop solving and do something else. Have a snack, watch TV, or play a game. When you return, you'll often find that you can solve the puzzle without any trouble. It's as if your brain just needed a break. It's also okay to look up answers in a dictionary, ask someone for help, or even take a peek (just a quick one) at the answers. Just remember to have fun!

On the Road

After you finish the crossword, read the circled letters only. Go from left to right and top to bottom to answer this riddle:

What do you say to a bunny who wants a ride?

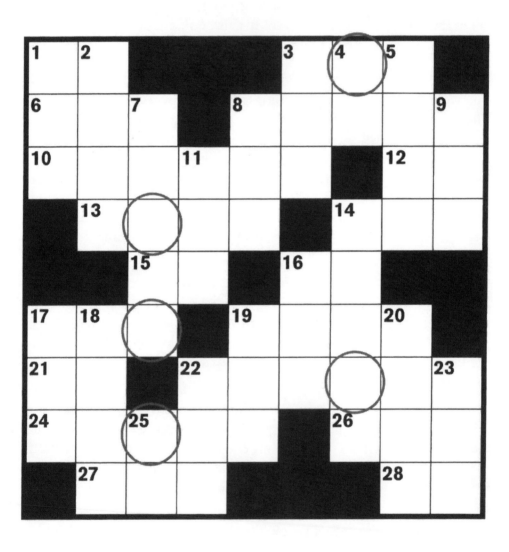

Across

1. Pa's wife
3. "Let's go to ___ park"
6. TV commercials
8. Sections
10. Yellow singing bird
12. Argentina's continent (abbr.)
13. Opposite of least
14. Phys. ed. classes are held here
15. Short form of Okay
16. Man's title (abbr.)
17. Police person
19. Bodies of water (sounds like SEIZE)
21. A tool used by a lumberjack
22. Storage rooms at the tops of houses
24. A one-cent coin
26. Short sleep
27. "No. I do ___ want any food."
28. The state next to New Jersey (abbr.)

Down

1. Type of computer made by Apple (short version)
2. Comic actor, ___ Sandler
3. Make an attempt to do something
4. Not she
5. Simple
7. Be very nosy and pry (rhymes with TROOP)
8. Paintings and sculpture are called ___
9. Dr. Seuss character, ___ I Am
11. ___ a question
14. Tiny particle of sand
16. Ran into
17. Baseball hat
18. Work animals with yokes around them
19. Pigpen
20. Use a special machine to read bar codes (rhymes with MAN)
22. Small insect that crawls
23. A secret agent like James Bond
25. Opposite of yes

Very Fishy

Each word in the list is also in the grid on the opposite page. Look up, down, and diagonally, both forward and backward, and circle each word when you find it. CARP is circled for you and crossed off the list. Then put the LEFTOVER LETTERS into the blanks below the grid. Work from left to right and top to bottom and you'll find the answer to this riddle:

What did one goldfish say to the other goldfish as they swam in the fishbowl?

~~CARP~~	SALMON
CISCO	SARDINE
COD	SHARK
EEL	SMELT
GUPPY	SNAPPER
HAKE	SOLE
LING	SPRAT
MARLIN	SWORDFISH
PICKEREL	TROUT
PIKE	TUNA
RAY	

8

L	I	N	G	R	A	Y	I	L	T
C	L	I	E	K	I	P	N	R	A
O	A	L	S	K	E	P	O	E	R
D	O	R	R	O	E	U	M	P	P
S	Y	A	P	C	T	G	L	P	S
O	H	M	U	S	U	A	A	A	M
S	A	R	D	I	N	E	S	N	E
R	K	O	U	C	A	N	E	S	L
L	E	R	E	K	C	I	P	L	T
D	H	S	I	F	D	R	O	W	S

🐷 **Riddle Answer:**

__ , __ __ __ __ __

__ __ __ __ __

9

Picture Crossword

Identify each picture and write its name in the proper place in the grid, going across or down. Then, read the circled boxes only. Go from left to right and top to bottom to answer this riddle:

What pierces your ears but doesn't leave a hole?

Across	Down
1.	1.
4.	2.
6.	3.
7.	4.
8.	5.
9.	8. **3**
11.	9.
13.	10.
15.	12.
16.	14.

Getting There

Each means of transportation will fit into one spot in the grid on the next page. Start with the letters that are already in the grid and work from there. When all the words are in the grid, place the starred letters in the blank spaces below. Go from left to right and top to bottom. You'll be able to finish this riddle:

What do travel agents say to their clients? Please . . .

3 Letters
BUS

CAB

JET

4 Letters
AUTO

JEEP

SHIP

5 Letters
BARGE

CANOE

KAYAK

KETCH

TRAIN

TRUCK

YACHT

6 Letters
CAMPER

JITNEY

SUBWAY

7 Letters
BICYCLE

SCOOTER

TRAWLER

TROLLEY

8 Letters
CABLE CAR

9 Letters
SUBMARINE

🐛 **Riddle Answer:**

__ __   __ __ __ __

Mouse Trap

After you finish the crossword, read the circled letters only. Go from left to right and top to bottom to answer this riddle:

What kind of royal cat is in a computer?

Across

1. To and __ (back and forth)
4. "What should we __ today?"
6. You use this to press clothes
7. A boy's name hidden in this word: MIRACLE
9. Facial features used for smelling
11. Baseball officials, for short
12. Atlanta's state (abbr.)
13. Type of dance
15. Opposite of her
17. The lobe is part of this
18. A green gem (rhymes with MADE)
19. Juicy fruit related to an orange
22. Small body of water
23. Someone who complains all the time is a ___
24. A guy who doesn't act like a gentleman (rhymes with FAD)
25. A tree with acorns
26. "Hello!"
28. Make a picture
30. Choose a President by voting
33. "Ready, __, go!"
34. A black-and-white sandwich cookie
35. The state next to Oregon (abbr.)
36. The supreme being who is worshiped

Down

1. Small animal that jumps
2. __ Parks, the civil rights activist
3. The number before two
4. Poorly lit (rhymes with RIM)
5. A child without any parents
6. Not out
8. Away or apart (anagram of ADE IS)
10. An adult male deer
11. Not down
14. Place where concerts are held
16. Not you
17. Finish
18. Irish dance
19. Warty creatures
20. President __ Jackson
21. Gardener's tool used to gather leaves
22. Desktop computer (abbr.)
25. "Ouch!"
26. A man who is very courageous
27. Frosted the cupcakes
29. A baby takes one step __ __ time
31. This is burned in a fireplace
32. "I want __ go home."

Fractured English

Put one of the words on this page into one of the blank spaces on the opposite page to make a sentence that makes sense if you're speaking fractured English. Read the sentences aloud for the best groaning effect! Each word will be used once, so you can cross it out when you've placed it in a spot. We did one for you.

ANTIDOTES

CANOE

COAX

DEVOTES

FLEECE

GEYSER

ILLEGAL

INSULATE

ORDER

PRAISE

RECEIPT

~~RECTOR~~

STUFF

SYMBOL

1. She <u>RECTOR</u> car and had it towed to the garage.

2. "I'll be happy to _____ you at another table," said the waiter.

3. The _____ on her nieces and nephews by spoiling them.

4. The campaign workers want to get out _____ for their candidate.

5. The _____ going to the beach with their girlfriends.

6. The mother yelled at her son because he came _____ from the party.

7. Do you want to buy the pink dress _____ blue one?

8. He did his homework quickly because it was so _____.

9. It _____ to find a good job.

10. The _____ was taken to the bird hospital for treatment.

11. The _____ in the woods bothered the hikers.

12. They served _____ and other soft drinks at the party.

13. _____ come to my birthday party?

14. The girl _____ in church every day.

Weighting Room

After you finish the crossword, read the circled letters only. Go from left to right and top to bottom to answer this riddle:

Where should a 300-pound monster go?

Across

1. Make a sound like a wild animal (rhymes with FOWL)
3. Person who imitates everything you do
8. A television show
9. Permit
10. Bright thoughts
11. Parties where people move to music
12. Shouts
14. Move around like a baby (rhymes with SLEEP)
17. The name of the "friendly ghost"
19. TV hostess, __ O'Donnell
22. Choose one or the __
23. People who give out cards in a game
24. Edges of a country
25. Pleased

Down

1. Merrily
2. Opposite of part
3. A show like "Malcolm in the Middle" is a situation __
4. The opposite of fancy
5. The school you attend after high school
6. Small city
7. Edges of the bread that you usually don't eat
13. Material used for shoes, belts, and jackets
14. A breakfast food like Rice Krispies
15. Ironed clothes
16. Grooms' wives
18. Lady's pocketbook
20. Say A-P-P-L-E for "apple"
21. Plastic object used to fix your hair

Don't Eat Your Veggies

Don't eat the veggies on this list! Instead, find each one in the grid on the opposite page. Look up, down, and diagonally both forward and backward and circle each one as you find it. Then, place the LEFT-OVER LETTERS into the spaces below the grid. Go from left to right and top to bottom and you'll find the answer to this riddle:

What vegetable is popular at the North Pole?

OKRA is circled and crossed off the list to get you started.

ASPARAGUS

BEAN

BEET

BROCCOLI

CABBAGE

CARROT

CHIVE

CORN

CUCUMBER

ESCAROLE

KALE

LEEK

MAIZE

~~OKRA~~

PEA

PEPPER

SORREL

SPINACH

SQUASH

```
I  R  E  B  M  U  C  U  C  B
C  C  E  B  E  S  O  R  E  R
H  G  E  L  Q  U  R  A  S  O
I  C  L  U  E  G  N  T  C  C
V  T  A  E  G  A  B  B  A  C
E  S  K  N  U  R  C  E  R  O
H  L  E  Z  I  A  M  E  O  L
R  E  P  P  E  P  E  T  L  I
L  E  R  R  O  S  S  A  E  P
(O  K  R  A)  C  A  R  R  O  T
```

🐝 **Riddle Answer:**

_ _ _ _ _ _   _ _ _ _ _ _ _

Cross Offs

Cross off each set of words described below. When you're finished, read the leftover words from left to right and top to bottom. They won't make any sense. But, if you change the first letter of each word you'll make a sentence that answers this riddle:

Why aren't grapes ever beaten up?

Cross off:

3 school subjects

5 names of U.S. Presidents

3 foreign cars

3 face parts

4 things you eat with a spoon

3 words that contain only the letters A, C, E, and R

2 girls' names

3 bodies of water

3 types of horses

Acre History NANCY Whey

Honda

Stallion Oatmeal

LIPS Lake Care Clinton

Math Bush RACE Gravel River

Kennedy Applesauce PONY

On Truman

TOYOTA Mary Soup

Volkswagen Hunches Pudding

EYES

Spelling Chin Reagan

Pond MARE

Staying Connected

Solve the crossword by writing the answer words in the correct spaces, going across or down. Next, look at each numbered line below the diagram. Find the letter that's in the same numbered square in the diagram and write it on the line. Read across to answer the riddle.

Where do spiders get their e-mail?

Across

1. Circle dance from Israel (rhymes with DORA)
5. Slightly wet
9. The upper crust of people (anagram of IT LEE)
11. Nut that comes from the oak tree
13. Body of water like the Mississippi
14. Type of race where a baton is passed from person to person
15. The little girl in "Uncle Tom's Cabin"
16. _____ a question
18. Material used to color Easter eggs
19. A fairy-tale creature
21. Cats and dogs are house ___
23. The place where football games are played
25. A singing bird
26. San Francisco ___ is a body of water (rhymes with SAY)
29. Abbr. for Individual Retirement Account
31. Lemon___ (refreshing summertime drink)
33. Big trouble (rhymes with TOE)
35. Slangy word for potato (rhymes with RATER)
37. "You can ___ ___ horse to water, but you can't make him drink"
39. Strain spaghetti in this (anagram of VEE IS)
40. Female horses
41. The slave, ___ Scott, took his case to the Supreme Court (rhymes with FRED)
42. If you ___ on someone, you can count on them

Down

1. Opposite of there
2. A green or black pitted item
3. A competitor
4. Had a meal
5. Turn black, like the sky
6. The highest playing card
7. Shapes
8. Do this in church
10. Important time period
12. Bill ____, the "Science Guy"
17. Use up money
20. Not close
22. The little thing on a file folder

24. Raised (children)
25. Liquid that comes out of a faucet
27. Knowing what's going on
28. Sing like a Swiss mountain person
29. "____ mine, not yours!"

30. A sudden, surprise attack (rhymes with MAID)
32. Type of shade tree
34. Simple
36. New Year's ___ is celebrated on Dec. 31
38. You hear with this

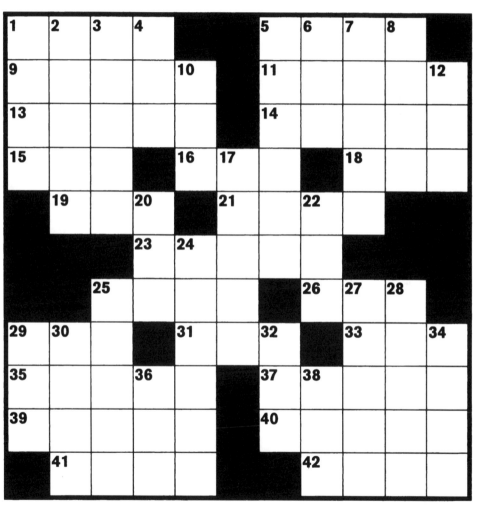

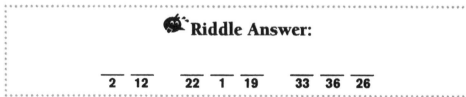

🐝 **Riddle Answer:**

 ___ ___   ___ ___ ___   ___ ___ ___
  2   12   22   1   19   33 36 26

Missing In Action

Fill in the missing letters in the grid below to make regular words reading across and down. Then move the filled-in letters to the identically numbered spaces below the grid to finish this riddle:

What job does the manager of the donut shop have?

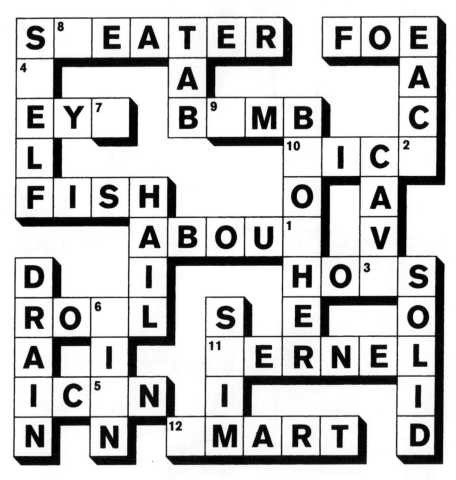

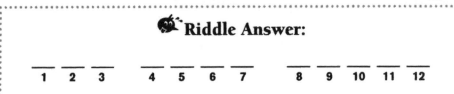

🍎 Riddle Answer:

___ ___ ___   ___ ___ ___ ___   ___ ___ ___ ___ ___
 1   2   3   4   5   6   7   8   9 10 11 12

More Missing In Action

Do the same thing on this page that you did on the opposite page to answer this riddle:

What side of the house does a cherry tree grow?

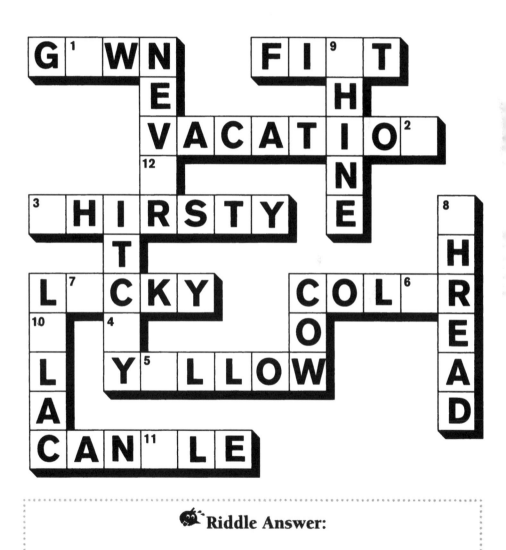

Three-Letter Pieces

All the answers to the clues below are in the box on the opposite page. Figure out the answer to each clue; then put two of the three-letter pieces together to make a six-letter word. Put the answer word into the diagram, writing DOWN. Since each piece will be used once, cross it out after you use it. When all the boxes have been filled in, read ACROSS the fourth row to answer this riddle:

What do you get if you cross a jogger with a beach?

Clues

1. Different from everything else

2. In a circle

3. Infants

4. Save from danger

5. Ruined by being smashed

6. The largest state of the U.S.A.

7. A shape with four equal sides

8. The meal that combines breakfast and lunch

9. The day before Tuesday

	1	2	3	4	5	6	7	8	9

*   *

ALA	CUE	QUE
ARE	DAY	RES
ARO	IES	SKA
BAB	KEN	SQU
BRO	MON	UND
BRU	NCH	UNI

Go With The Flow

Fill in the grid with words that answer the clues, both across and down. Next, fill in the numbered lines with the letters that are written in the matching numbered squares. Third, read across to answer this riddle:

What kind of pool can't you swim in?

Across

1. Carpets
5. Pretend
8. It's polite to write __ __ of thanks for a gift
10. Proof of ownership for a homeowner (rhymes with SEED)
12. "Please don't leave yet. __ __ few minutes more."
13. Stranger
14. Smack
15. Be in a race
17. "Have you __ wool?"
18. The 19th letter
20. Marks that show you've had an operation
22. "Do you want one or the __?"
24. Comic-strip, "Little Orphan __"
26. Fast, faster, fast__
29. Long, long __ (the past)
30. A married woman's title (abbr.)
32. __meal, hot cereal
34. Fur used for coats (rhymes with FABLE)

36. The first word you say when you answer the phone
38. Heap
39. Fairy-tale creatures who help Santa make toys
40. Hit the ball over a __ in volleyball
41. "Clean up this room. It's a __!" (rhymes with BESS)

Down

1. People with allergies may break out in a __
2. Take apart shoelaces (anagram of UNITE)
3. Farm animals with beards
4. Hog's home
5. Opposite of subtract
6. Nice-smelling wood used in closets
7. People between the ages of 13 and 19
9. In one __ and out the other
11. Use a towel to __ yourself
13. "__ upon a time"
16. This person will seat you in a theater
19. A male child is a __

21. Kid's book, "__ You My Mother?"
23. Use a wristwatch to tell __
24. Once more
25. Very impressive (anagram of LO BEN)
27. Do a crossword puzzle

28. Fairy __ (rhymes with BALES)
29. Serpent
31. The girl
33. Throw a ball
35. Permit
37. Shade tree

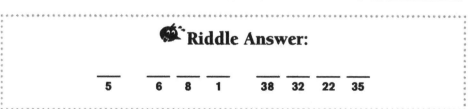

Riddle Answer:

____ ____ ____ ____   ____ ____ ____ ____
 5   6   8   1   38   32   22   35

Arrow Words #1

In this crossword the clues are written inside the grid. Follow the directions of the arrows and write each answer word in the blank spaces going across or down.

Opposite of worst	Opposite of west	Opposite of fast	Cab	Bump on the skin	▼	First number	Had a meal	Move your head
▶	▼	▼	▼	Money that is borrowed ▶		▼	▼	▼
Pie ___ ___ mode ▶				Go ___ the house ▶				
Boston Red ___ ▶				Plant this Iowa is one ▶				
Hurt an ankle by turning it ▶				▼		Latest events	Click your fingers	Simple
Obtain	Breakfast food	Also	Uptight ▶			▼	▼	▼
▶	▼	▼	Stadium ___ apple a day ▶					
Farm animal ▶			▼		Used to be ▶			
Missing ▶					Movie "___ Kids" ▶			

32

Just Joking #1

Fill in the blanks on each line to spell the name of a mammal. Then read down the starred column to answer this riddle:

What should you do with a blue elephant?

```
                *
      P O R _ U P I N E
          _ A M S T E R
      A N T _ L O P E
        H Y _ N A
        B U _ R O

          C _ E E T A H
      S Q U _ R R E L
      L L A _ A

    C H I P M _ N K
          _ A N T H E R
```

Camping Out

After you finish the crossword, read the circled letters only. Go from left to right and top to bottom to finish this riddle:

Where do baby dogs sleep when they go camping? In . . .

Across

1. You wear this on your head
4. Had a snack
7. Car- __ (shared the driving with other people)
10. "Once __ a time. . ."
11. The referee in a baseball game
12. Use the mail system to __ a letter
13. Clothing chain found in most malls, The __
14. Fix potatoes (rhymes with BASH)
16. Not he
17. Fib
18. Comic actor, __ Sandler
21. High-school dance, the senior __
24. Like two peas in a __
26. Noisy group of people
28. Rain hard (sounds like POOR)
30. Female sheep (sounds like YOU)
31. A hammer or saw is a __
34. Dirtied (rhymes with BOILED)
36. Become smaller, like the moon (rhymes with PANE)
37. These are used in printers (rhymes with LONERS)
38. What a miner mines
39. A small rug

Down

1. Moved like a bunny
2. Famous boxer, Muhammad __
3. A school semester is also a __ (rhymes with GERM)
4. Monkey
5. One __ equals 2,000 pounds
6. Opposite of start
7. Dogs with wrinkled faces (rhymes with MUGS)
8. A city in Nebraska
9. Pass out the playing cards
10. A man who seats you at a wedding
15. Use a straw to __ a drink
19. Popular red fruit
20. The sound made by a cow
22. An egg dish that is filled with ham, cheese, or veggies
23. Cut the grass with a lawn __
25. Use a __ cloth to clean the furniture
27. Sleeping places
29. The living __ is part of the house
31. The number before three
32. Use an __ to move a boat
33. The first number
35. "We'll be there __ __ second."

Baked Goodies

Why did the robber hold up the bakery?

To find the answer to this riddle, put each bakery product into the grid on the opposite page. Use the letters that are already there PLUS the length of each word to guide you. When you're done, read down the starred column. You'll "TURNOVER" with laughter!

BISCUIT

BRIOCHE

BROWNIE

CAKE

CHEESE CAKE

COBBLER

COOKIE

CRULLER

DANISH

DOUGHNUT

ECLAIR

GINGERBREAD

MUFFIN

PIE

SHORTCAKE

STRUDEL

TURNOVER

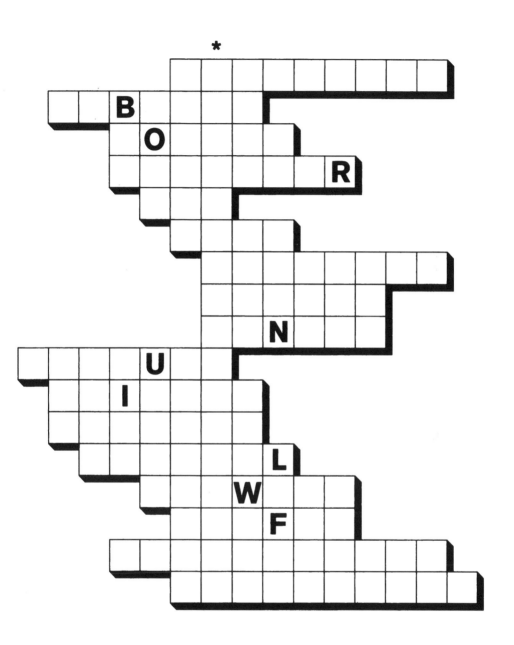

Family Byes

After you finish the crossword, read the circled letters only. Go from left to right and top to bottom to answer this riddle:

What did the daddy buffalo say to his child when he went to school?

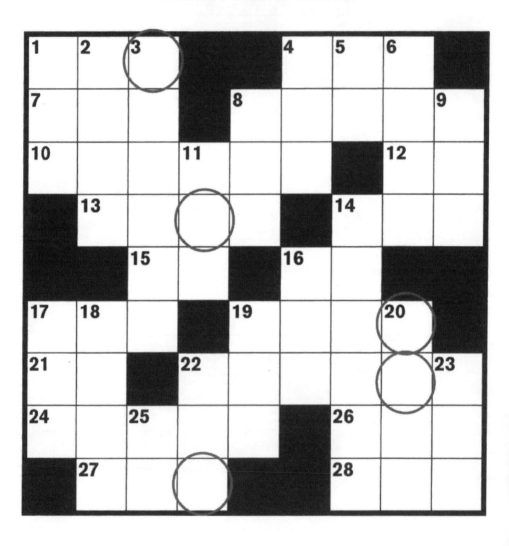

Across

1. A small lie is a __
4. America's Uncle __
7. This card is higher than a king
8. Popular Mexican food
10. Had to have
12. "__ my! I'm so surprised!"
13. Twirl around
14. Some
15. Nickname for Edward
16. Abbr. for railroad
17. Very angry
19. Edges
21. Opposite of down
22. Listening devices on car dashboards
24. Postponement (rhymes with RELAY)
26. A large deer with antlers
27. __ Francisco, California
28. Type of sauce used on sushi

Down

1. Cooling device
2. You might eat Italian __ on a hot day
3. Used a pager to contact someone
4. Opposite of happy
5. Abbr. for air conditioning
6. A heavenly body seen in the night sky
8. The number after nine
9. Timid
11. Past of do
14. Groups of soldiers
16. "Get __ of this junk! Throw it out!"
17. Wet dirt
18. Monkeys
19. A beam of light
20. A person who performs alone is doing a __
22. Was in a marathon
23. The upper atmosphere
25. Abbr. for Los Angeles

It's A Crime . . .

. . . to put such outrageous rhymes into this book. But, that's not stopping us.

Each line contains a nonsense phrase that rhymes with the name of someone famous. The answer could be a real person, a group, a cartoon character, or something else! Read each phrase out loud (please, whisper so no one else will hear you) and write the real name on the blanks. There are clues on the opposite page to help you identify each one.

1. TOWER MUFF PEARLS   _____

2. PLANET LACKS TON   _____

3. PAL MORE   _____

4. BARON BARTER   _____

5. PICKY HOUSE   _____

6. GORY SHELLING   _____

7. HACK GREET TOYS   _____

8. MILL DATES   _____

9. BUST IN LIMBER BAKE   _____

10. TIA JAM   _____

11. MUGS FUNNY   _____

12. CREW LARRY CORE   _____

13. SPOT HOLEY   _____

14. PONY GAWK   _____

15. SASSY   _____

Hints

1. Crime-fighting cartoon group
2. Singer who comes from a large musical family
3. Bill Clinton's vice-president
4. A singer whose brother is a member of #7
5. Star of Walt Disney's empire
6. "90210" actress whose father is a famous producer
7. Male singing group
8. The head of Microsoft and one of the richest people in the world
9. Member of *NSync
10. Famous female soccer player
11. Cartoon character whose favorite words are "What's up, Doc?"
12. Actress whose first movie was "E.T."
13. Actor who stars on "Felicity"
14. One of the greatest skateboarders ever
15. Four-legged movie and TV star

Daffynition

Solve the crossword by answering each clue and writing it in the grid, going across and down. Then, read only the circled letters from left to right and top to bottom to find the word that has this meaning:

The penalty you pay for going over the feed limit.

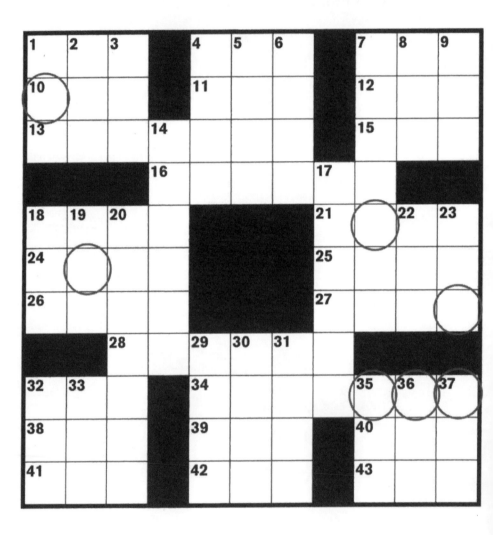

Across

1. You can draw and paint in
   __ class
4. Kids' book, "Hop on __"
7. Use a straw to take a __ of
   soda
10. A female deer
11. Go __ __ trip (travel)
12. Tangy drink, lemon__
13. Horses' homes on a farm
15. Use oars to move a boat
16. Took a break from working
18. Plus
21. Plate
24. Hide and __ is a popular
    game
25. Go __ the room
26. In this place
27. Exam
28. Immediately! (anagram of
    NOR TOP)
32. "Beauty and __ Beast"
34. Raining very hard
38. Nickname for President
    Reagan
39. Broad street (abbr.)
40. Type of sauce used on chow
    mein
41. "Are We There __?"
42. __ Vegas is a city in Nevada
43. Body part that goes through
    a sleeve

Down

1. Commercials, for short
2. Go bad, like food
3. Drink that has its own "bag"
4. The North __ is a cold place
5. Dollar bills are called __
6. If it happened a while ago;
   it's in the __
7. Small fish that's packed
   tightly in a can
8. What a bride says at the altar
   (2 words)
9. A seat in a church
14. A real-estate __ might sell
    your house (rhymes with
    JOKER)
17. A worker at a magazine or
    newspaper
18. A small bit of fireplace stuff
19. Movie director, Spike __
20. A large poisonous snake
    (anagram of NEST REP)
22. City roads are called __(abbr.)
23. Opposite of cold
29. The birthstone for October
    (anagram of PALO)
30. __ Scotia is in Canada
31. The day after Monday (abbr.)
32. Make an attempt to do
    something
33. Tool for weeding
35. She __ __ good teacher
36. Country next to Sweden
    (abbr.)
37. Phys. ed. classes take place
    here

Find The Riddle

Here's the answer to a riddle:

They wanted a coffee break.

Before you start laughing you'll have to find the riddle. Do these things:

Figure out the answer to each clue
Write the answer word in the numbered spaces
Write the same letter on the same numbered space on the opposite page
Work back and forth between both pages

Clues

Opposite of dry

___ ___ ___
 1   5   8

The capital of Italy

___ ___ ___ ___
13   25   35   29

The color of clouds

___ ___ ___ ___ ___
 4   9   19   27   31

Opposite of back

___ ___ ___ ___ ___
18   6   12   38   30

This opens a lock

___ ___ ___
14   21   39

Uncooked

___ ___ ___
24   37   11

Use this to water the lawn

___ ___ ___ ___
 2   34   17   7

Give nourishment to a baby

___ ___ ___ ___
23   15   10   22

Be nosy (rhymes with dry)

___ ___ ___
36   16   3

A small object on a bracelet

___ ___ ___ ___ ___
33   28   32   20   26

Riddle:

$\overline{}_{1}$ $\overline{}_{2}$ $\overline{}_{3}$ $\overline{}_{4}$ $\overline{}_{5}$ $\overline{}_{6}$ $\overline{}_{7}$ $\overline{}_{8}$ $\overline{}_{9}$ $\overline{}_{10}$

$\overline{}_{11}$ $\overline{}_{12}$ $\overline{}_{13}$ $\overline{}_{14}$ $\overline{}_{15}$ $\overline{}_{16}$ $\overline{}_{17}$ $\overline{}_{18}$ $\overline{}_{19}$ $\overline{}_{20}$ $\overline{}_{21}$ $\overline{}_{22}$

$\overline{}_{23}$ $\overline{}_{24}$ $\overline{}_{25}$ $\overline{}_{26}$ $\overline{}_{27}$ $\overline{}_{28}$ $\overline{}_{29}$ $\overline{}_{30}$ $\overline{}_{31}$ $\overline{}_{32}$

$\overline{}_{33}$ $\overline{}_{34}$ $\overline{}_{35}$ $\overline{}_{36}$ $\overline{}_{37}$ $\overline{}_{38}$ $\overline{}_{39}$?

Up In The Air

Fill in the grid with words that answer the clues, both across and down. Next, fill in the numbered lines with the letters that are written in the matching numbered squares. Then, read across to finish this riddle:

If farmers can raise tons of crops in dry weather, what can they raise in wet weather?

Riddle Answer:

$\overline{33}$ $\overline{23}$ $\overline{32}$ $\overline{39}$ $\overline{26}$ $\overline{25}$ $\overline{22}$ $\overline{5}$ $\overline{8}$

Across

1. Spinning toy
4. One of your parents
7. Opposite of takes
9. Adult female
11. Play football games in an __
12. "What __ __ baby! She's so adorable!"
13. MPH means miles __ hour
14. Old broken-down horse is a __ (rhymes with GAG)
16. "Ready, __, go!"
17. Very unhappy
19. Rounded roofs like the one on the U.S. Capitol building
21. Without any other person
23. The head elected person in a city
25. Allow
28. __ and vinegar are used on salads
29. The day after Tuesday (abbr.)
31. A noisy crowd that's hard to control
33. Join together in a union
35. Overact, like an actor who's a ham (anagram of ME TOE)
37. Name for a dog
38. Healed a patient
39. The color of blood
40. The place where athletes work out

Down

1. There are four of these on a car
2. If you're __ __ barrel, you're in a lot of trouble
3. Use this to sign a check
4. Bugs Bunny says, "What's Up, __?"
5. Entertain someone
6. Goes out with someone (rhymes with GATES)
7. Store that sells jeans and tops, The __
8. California city, __ Diego
9. A child's toy with wheels
10. This divides a tennis court
15. Be extremely fond of someone
18. A 24-hour period
20. Movie star, __ Gibson
22. Opposite of higher
23. A person under the age of 18 is a __
24. Not dead
26. A college in Atlanta, Georgia (anagram of MY ORE)
27. A tribal symbol, the __ pole
28. Not their
30. The last month of the year (abbr.)
32. Sleeping place
34. Senator __ Kennedy
36. Large drinking cup

This Is A Frame-up!

Take a break and solve this "fake" puzzle! It's just a frame-up because there are only words on the frame of the grid. Fill in this frame with words that match the clues below. Each word shares 1, 2, or 3 letters with the one that comes after it. Start each word in the same space as its clue number. When you get to a corner, follow the direction of the arrow. Since this is meant to be easy, there are more hints for you on the opposite page. Remember, an anagram is a rearrangement of the letters of one word or phrase for another word or phrase, like STREAM and MASTER.

Clues

1. Astronauts travel in outer __.

2. Portable phones are called __ phones.

3. A train that makes all the stops is a __.

4. A chart that shows a whole year's worth of dates is a __.

5. A story in a newspaper is an __.

6. Someone who has a quick mind is __.

7. Poetry is also called __.

8. Quite a few.

9. Opposite of never.

10. The body organ where food starts to digest is the __.

11. A martial arts expert might give someone a karate __.

12. Opposite of shut.

13. Go inside (a house).

14. A floor that slopes and is used by people in wheelchairs is a __.

15. Opposite of pull.

16. A vehicle used by astronauts.

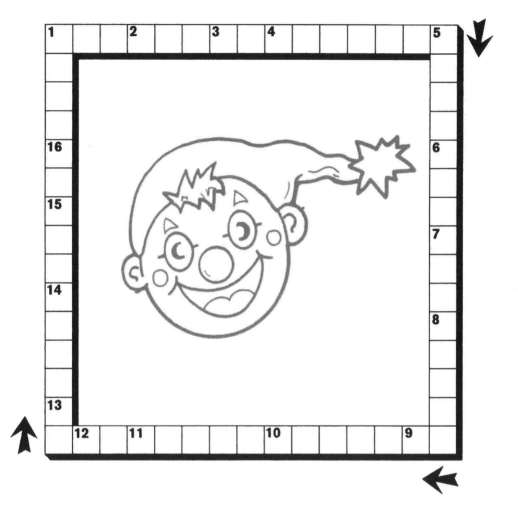

Hints

1. Rhymes with race
2. Rhymes with bell
3. Rhymes with vocal
4. Anagram of CARD LANE
5. Anagram of IT CLEAR
6. Rhymes with ever
7. Anagram of SEVER
8. An anagram of AL VEERS
9. An anagram of SAY LAW
10. An anagram of HAM COTS
11. Rhymes with shop
12. Anagram of NOPE
13. Rhymes with renter
14. Rhymes with damp
15. Rhymes with bush
16. Anagram of HIPS

Oh My!

Every word in this list starts with the letter "O." OWL is circled to start you off. After you find and circle each of the 15 other words, put the UNUSED letters into the spaces below the grid. Go from left to right and top to bottom and you'll find the answer to this riddle:

How many letters are in the alphabet?
(Hint: it's not what you think it is!)

OARS

OASIS

OBOE

OBSERVE

OCCUPY

ODOR

OFFENSIVE

OFFERED

OFFICE

OFFSET

OILY

OLIVE

OOZE

OPINION

OVENS

~~OWL~~

O D O R

O F F S E T

O P F S I S A O

C I E F E O B O

E C N N O E S S W L

E U I S A E R N L E

P O I R V V E E

Y N V S I N V D

E E Y L I O

E Z O O

_ _ _ _ _ _

Pop Rock

Fill in the grid with words that answer the clues, both across and down. Next, fill in the numbered lines with the letters that are written in the matching numbered squares. Then, read across to answer this riddle:

What do you get if you cross a CD player with a refrigerator?

Across

1. Glass container for mayonnaise
4. A group for members only
8. Ocean liner
12. Nickname for President Lincoln
13. Be fond of someone
14. A bee's home (rhymes with DIVE)
15. You sleep on this
16. Not closed
17. A sign of the future
18. __ down (gets ready to stop)
20. Mix (batter)
22. The bottom part of a dress
24. Homes for birds
28. Be passionate about
31. Not brand-new
34. Fib

35. Bake a pie in this
36. Cover of a pot
37. Arrived
38. Used a chair
39. "__ you in school yesterday?"
40. Monkeys
41. Go down a ski __ (rhymes with ROPE)
43. This divides a tennis court
45. Male person who inherits money
48. Specks in the fireplace from burning wood
52. Bread with a "pocket" (rhymes with RITA)
55. Winter jacket
57. "How __ you feeling today?"
58. Important time periods
59. Rim
60. Tear
61. Use Scotch __ instead of glue
62. An animal like Bambi
63. Ran into

Down
1. Pokes with the elbow
2. The brother of Cain in the Bible
3. Decorate once more
4. Nearby
5. Half of the mouth
6. Instruments that are like guitars
7. __ down and stooped (rhymes with DENT)
8. The seacoast (rhymes with MORE)
9. That boy
10. Contraction meaning "I have"
11. A writing tool filled with ink
19. "At what time?"
21. The state next to Ohio (abbr.)
23. Stubborn as a __
25. Hit someone hard
26. "What __ is it?"
27. Looks at
28. Opposite of profit
29. The shape of an egg
30. The President has a right to do this to a bill (anagram of VOTE)
32. Title of respect for a man
33. Adam and Eve lived in the garden of __
37. Animals that meow
39. Very tiny
42. Aspect (anagram of SHAPE)
44. "Peter, Peter, pumpkin __"
46. Frosted a cake
47. Went by car
49. Hurt
50. One of the Great Lakes
51. The month after August (abbr.)
52. A gerbil could be a house __
53. A man's name (anagram of ARI)
54. Knock gently
56. Get old

Crowd Control

This puzzle is popping out at 30 Across, just like a stadium with an overflow crowd. Can you fill in all the blanks and find the four-word phrase to describe this situation?

Across

1. One turn around a race circuit is a __ (rhymes with NAP)
4. The month after September (abbr.)
7. Tall shade tree
10. An __ cube makes drinks cold
11. To and __ (back and forth)
12. Opposite of under
13. People drink this instead of coffee
14. A warty creature that's like a frog
16. Stops working, like a battery
17. Pop out, like lava from a volcano (rhymes with CHEW)

19. A person who is worshiped
21. Raggedy __ and Andy are cloth dolls
22. Black goo used to pave roads
23. Sound made by a lion
26. Do the same work as Jennifer Love Hewitt
27. Singing sounds, __ la la
30. Be overcrowded (4 words)
34. Popular chain of clothing stores, The __
35. Not he
36. Memorial Day race, the __ 500
37. Go down slopes on runners
38. The ocean on the west coast of the USA (abbr.)
40. Popular sport, __ball
41. Materials in pens
43. Twirl around
45. Wave a — at an Independence Day parade
47. Ancient
50. An evergreen tree with needles
51. The number before two
52. What you breathe
53. Opposite of no
54. The word used with neither
55. Open a locked door with this

Down

1. Illuminated
2. Highest playing card
3. These veggies go with carrots
4. Frequently
5. "Jack fell down and broke his __"
6. "Do you want to go __ __ movie?"
7. Very bad
8. Movie director Spike __
9. Robin Williams' movie, "__ Doubtfire"
12. Smell
15. Long and narrow hole (rhymes with PITCH)
18. Piece
20. Sticky fruit from a palm tree
23. Floor covering
24. "Are you a man __ __ mouse?"
25. A deadly snake (anagram of SPA)
26. Had food
27. Six + four = __
28. Something fab is __ (rhymes with BAD)
29. Singer __ Grant
31. Opposite of tells
32. Someone who steals is a __
33. Not healthy
37. Not crazy
38. An instrument with a key-board
39. Rage
40. Coal holders
42. Keep something in water for a long time
43. A secret agent
44. Dessert with a crust
46. Former actor who played monster roles, __ Chaney
48. Fib
49. Opposite of wet

House Business?

Each house part will fit into one spot in the grid on the opposite page. Start by placing DEN (the only three-letter word) into the grid and work from there. Be careful because there are some tricky spots. When all the words are in the grid, read the circled letters from left to right and top to bottom to answer this riddle:

What clothing does a house wear?

3 Letters

DEN

4 Letters

BATH

ROOF

YARD

5 Letters

ATTIC

FOYER

PATIO

6 Letters

CELLAR

CLOSET

OFFICE

PANTRY

7 Letters

BALCONY

BEDROOM

CARPORT

DINETTE

KITCHEN

LAUNDRY

LIBRARY

NURSERY

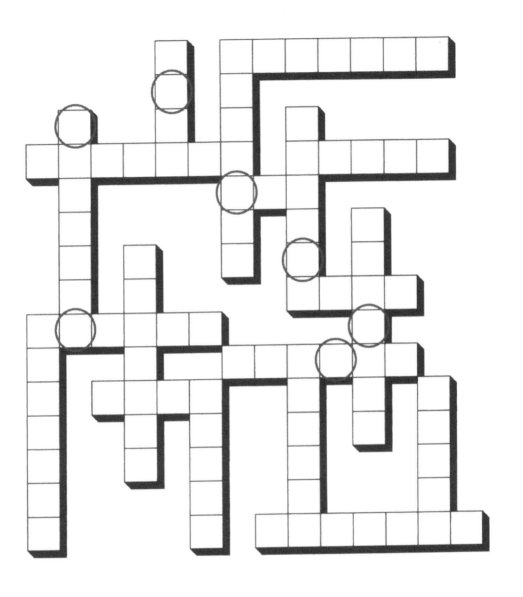

Computer Confusion

Where do messy computer operators store their information?

To find the answer to this riddle, circle each of the synonyms for messy that are listed below. Look up, down, and diagonally, both forward and backward in the grid on the opposite page. Then put the LEFTOVER LETTERS into the spaces underneath the grid. Go from left to right and top to bottom. Laugh out loud when you're done!

ASKEW

AWRY

CARELESS

DISORDERLY

ERRATIC

HAPHAZARD

IRREGULAR

LOOSE

MESSY

MUDDLED

RANDOM

SLACK

SLIPSHOD

TOPSY-TURVY

UPSET

```
D O H S P I L S O Y
R I R R E G U L A R
A E S O O L N S D W
Z R L O U P S E T A
A R C A R E L E S S
H A R A N D O M O L
P T P P D W E K S A
A I Y U D I S R K C
H C M E S S Y S L K
T O P S Y T U R V Y
```

Five 5 x 5's

There are five similar things hidden in each little grid on these two pages. To find them, you'll have to pick one letter from each column, going from left to right. Each letter will be used once, so cross it off after you use it. The category for each grouping is written above the grid. We did the first one for you.

Animals

1. <u>H O R S E</u>

2. _____

3. _____

4. _____

5. _____

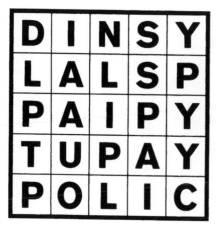

Flowers

1. _____

2. _____

3. _____

4. _____

5. _____

S	T	Y	L	N
I	P	P	I	A
E	H	A	P	Y
C	A	A	N	T
J	G	I	A	N

Foreign Countries

1. _____
2. _____
3. _____
4. _____
5. _____

B	E	P	P	Y
A	E	A	C	N
P	P	M	O	E
G	E	A	L	E
L	R	R	R	H

Fruits

1. _____
2. _____
3. _____
4. _____
5. _____

F	A	L	L	O
P	E	A	T	N
B	I	N	N	O
O	R	U	J	E
C	L	G	A	O

Musical Instruments

1. _____
2. _____
3. _____
4. _____
5. _____

Night Mare?

When the crossword is solved, fill in the numbered spaces below the grid with the letters in the same numbered squares to answer this riddle:

Who always goes to bed with shoes on?

🐴 **Riddle Answer:**

___ ___ ___ ___ ___ ___
6   9   27   7   25 30

Across

1. Someone who is very formal is __ (rhymes with TRIM)
5. Send a sick person a Get Well __
9. Type of collision where two cars hit each other in the front (hyphenated word)
11. Busy as __ __
12. Area in a mall where kids play video games
13. A method of doing something
14. Go down snowy slopes
15. Spring holiday celebrated on a Sunday
17. Addition columns: ones, __, hundreds
19. "Let's go __ __ movie."
20. Rims
22. Dog attacks
26. Also
28. The longest river in the world (rhymes with PILE)
29. Arises from bed (2 words)
32. Term of address for a holy person (abbr.)
33. Own
34. Put tar on the road again
36. "They lived happily __ after."
37. This insect sat down beside Miss Muffet
38. Sloppy area with things lying around
39. "I lost my book. Have you __ it?"

Down

1. __ up (got more lively; rhymes with JERKED)
2. Running in a marathon
3. The state next to Wyoming (abbr.)
4. Brownie a la __ (with ice cream)
5. The person in charge of a ship
6. Ready, willing, and __
7. "Step to the __ of the bus!" (the back)
8. A cozy room in a house
9. An old saying, "__ makes waste"
10. Very organized with everything in its place
16. Cry
18. Irish __ (long-haired hunting dogs)
21. Urgent message sent by ships in trouble (abbr.)
23. An angry outburst (anagram of DIE RAT)
24. One less than a dozen
25. Cut off (rhymes with NEVER)
27. Belonging to us
29. Opposite of took
30. The nights before holidays
31. __ up and becomes energetic (rhymes with REPS)
33. The bottom part of a skirt
35. A dessert with a crust and filling

Weather Report

After you finish the crossword, read the circled letters only. Go from left to right and top to bottom to answer this riddle:

If it's raining cats and dogs, what does a vet step into?

Across

1. Medical wrappings for cuts and wounds
5. A body of water that sounds like 27 Across
7. President Lincoln's nickname
8. Large cup for coffee
9. Drink with a straw and make lots of noise
10. The opposite of buy
11. Make a sweater with yarn and 2 Down
12. Not against
14. Glued
15. Summer is the warmest __ of the year
18. "Hansel __ Gretel"
20. Belonging to us
21. Opposite of short
24. It comes before fourth
25. Fourth letter of the alphabet
26. An octopus squirts this stuff
27. The letter after B
28. Happy events starring brides and grooms

Down

1. Poorly behaved kids like Dennis the Menace
2. Pointy objects used to make sweaters
3. Group of soldiers
4. Motor
5. Cram things into a small space
6. What an adult might take for a headache
9. A baby __ watches children
13. This follows first
14. Synthetic material for gallon containers of milk
16. Place where trains arrive and leave, railroad __
17. Rocking bed for an infant
19. Use a steering wheel to __ a car
22. Bodies of water like Erie, Huron, Michigan, etc.
23. One of the round objects on a necklace

First/Last

Rearrange the letters of each of these common words to make another common word without adding or taking away any letters. For example, LEAF can be rearranged to make FLEA. Write the new word in the grid on the opposite page. Some words will end at the starred column and others will begin there. When you're done, read down the starred column to find the two-word answer to this riddle:

What vehicle would be used to take a sick pig to the hospital?

1. LEAF

2. HARE

3. AIDE

4. LIME

5. CABS

6. SUES

7. EARL

8. PEAS

9. BRAN

10. TACO

11. PACE

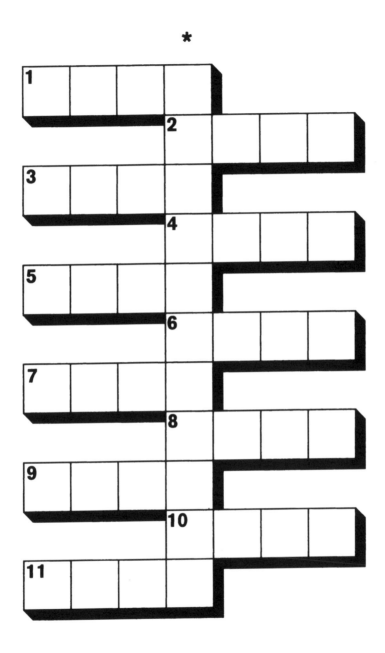

Piece Of The Pie?

Fill in the grid with words that answer the clues, both across and down. Next, fill in the numbered lines with the letters that are written in the matching numbered squares. Then, read across to answer this riddle:

What happens to pizza when it's 3,000 years old?

Across

1. George Washington was the first __ of the U.S.
6. Unhappy
8. Exhausted
9. Places where flowers grow
10. Polite word used when you ask for something
12. Mistake
13. A person who uses a keyboard
15. Real __ agent
18. Large deer with an antler
20. Use this to keep a ship at dock
23. Opposite of shortest
24. "Don't be a sore __ if you don't win."
26. "What __ you do last summer?"
27. When you get a __, your loafers or oxfords get polished

Down

1. __ down (places in a spot)
2. Hearing organ
3. New Delhi is the capital of this country
4. American birds are called __
5. Birds associated with Thanksgiving
6. "Do you __ to tell the whole truth?"
7. Merit (rhymes with RESERVE)
11. A toddler likes to sit on Mom's __
13. Lost one's balance and fell (rhymes with RUMBLED)
14. Hear music on these machines
16. Long, long __
17. Fidel __ is the leader of Cuba
19. Possessed
21. Prisoners live in jail __
22. Not costing anything
25. Do a winter sport on snow

Riddle Answer:

___ ___   ___ ___ ___ ___   ___ ___ ___ ___
3   8   9   12 13 14   17 19 24 26

Hue Said It

There are no gimmicks to this puzzle. All you have to do is fill in the blanks with words that fit the clues. There are lots of color words, so you can use a crayon instead of a pencil!

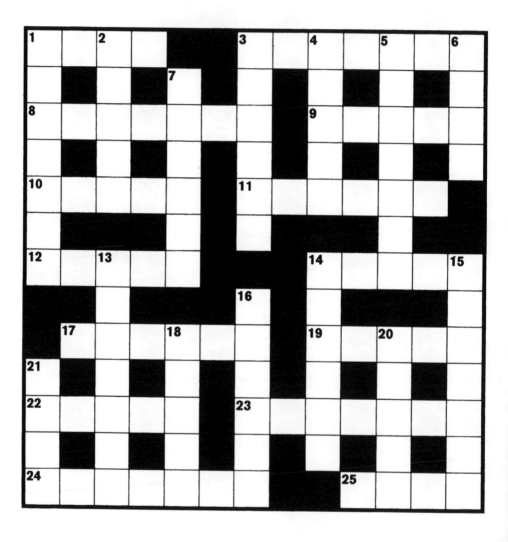

Across

1. Neutral color that's a mixture of black and white
3. Makes different
8. Purplish-red color (anagram of GATEMAN)
9. The color of grass
10. A shade of purple that's also a flower
11. Oil
12. The bottom parts of flowers
14. Spaghetti and macaroni are types of __
17. A ten-year period
19. Sweet-smelling flowers with thorns (or, shades of red)
22. Precise
23. Blow this up at a party
24. F.B.I. stands for __ Bureau of Investigation
25. Color of the ocean

Down

1. Tries to win money in casinos
2. Heavenly creature with a halo
3. Use a credit card to __ something
4. Quarrel with someone
5. Makes estimates
6. Basin in a bathroom or kitchen
7. Raps on a door before entering
13. Shade of green that's also a jewel
14. The color of grapes
15. Proverb, "__ makes the heart grow fonder" (opposite of PRESENCE)
16. Furry animal that's like a mouse
18. Brad Pitt is a popular __
20. Thread is wound on this
21. Not able to hear

Game Plan

This is a game where the last letter of one word is also the first letter of the next word. All the last/first letters are in the grid. Answer the first clue and write it in the grid, starting with the T in the top left box. Next, answer the second clue that starts with the S at the end of the first word. Continue doing this as you go across, down, up, and backward through the diagram. The last word will be related to the first word.

A game played by Venus Williams

Buy things in a store

Not having enough money

Having loads of money

The "middle" of a donut

The joint between your upper and lower arm

Opposite of dry

The number before three

Opposite of young

Student's table in a classroom

Baby goats

Carpenter's cutting tool

"Which person?"

Seven is an __ number

The person who operates a car

Take stuff illegally, like a thief

Sound made by a bee

A metal that is used in brass

"Peanuts" is a __ strip feature found in newspapers

The place where Andre Agassi plays his game

Arrow Words #2

In this crossword the clues are written inside the grid. Follow the directions of the arrows and write each answer word in the blank spaces going across or down.

Get taller	Tool for gathering leaves	Not shut	___ away (left)	Hosed the plants	▼	Polish the floor	___ Baba & the 40 thieves	Still
▶	▼	▼	▼	Go ___ (leave) ▶		▼	▼	▼
Monkey ▶				Fairy ___ ▶				
Barbie's boyfriend ▶				Opposite of go in ▶				
Go inside ▶				Wipe out ▼		Former V.P. Al ___	Press clothes	Mail out
Wild animal park	Not on	Grease	Host ___ Philbin ▶			▼	▼	▼
▶	▼	▼	Love a lot ▶ Can that ___ true?					
Lies ▶			▼		Ronald's nickname ▶			
Run away ▶					Opposite of start ▶			

74

Just Joking #2

Fill in the blanks on each line to spell the name of something associated with outer space. Then read down the starred column to answer this riddle:

Where do alien dentists live?

*

JUP __ TER

__ EPTUNE

SA __ URN

EART __

V __ NUS

__ ERCURY

PLUT __

SATE __ LITE

M __ RS

U __ ANUS

__ TAR

GALAX __

__ UN

AS __ EROID

M __ TEOR

__ OON

Hidden Birds

Each sentence has the name of a bird hidden between two or more words. For example, SWAN is hidden in 1 Across. First, underline the name of each bird. Second, write its name in the diagram starting in the matching numbered square. Third, put a feather in your cap when you're finished.

Across

1. HE'S <u>WAN</u>DERING AWAY.

5. HERE'S THE CHAPEL I CAN ATTEND.

8. CAN A RYE BREAD BE USED FOR TOAST?

9. SAY HELLO ONCE MORE.

10. DO VERY RICH PEOPLE LIKE BARGAINS?

11. HOW LOVELY YOU LOOK!

13. GIVE THE HERO BING CHERRIES.

14. DO YOU LIKE THE OBOIST OR KAZOO PLAYER BEST?

15. MR. SHAW KISSED HIS WIFE.

Down

2. WE'LL NOW RENEW OUR SUBSCRIPTIONS.

3. I HAVE A GLEN PLAID SUIT.

4. THE MOVIE STAR LINGERED TO TALK TO HIS FANS.

6. LET ME KNOW IF AL CONDUCTS THE TOUR.

7. IS HER CONDO RIGHT NEXT TO YOURS?

10. DO DOGS LIKE BONES?

12. NOAH HAD A SMALL ARK.

Double Cross (word)

You'll find the answers to two riddles here. So you can have twice as much fun solving!

Across

1. High card
4. A girl's name that rhymes with JAM
7. The color of strawberries
10. A 24-hour period
11. Take one step __ __ time
12. Contraction for I HAVE
13. WHAT CONTEST DID THE WITCH WIN? A __ __
16. Plenty (rhymes with SAMPLE)
17. Hits with the hand
20. Ingredient in bread that makes it rise
24. Knock gently on a door
25. Civil War general, Robert E. __
26. The opposite of sour
29. Food made with tomatoes, lettuce, peppers, onions
31. Items used for washing
33. WHAT DID THE MOTHER LIGHTNING BUG SAY ABOUT HER SON? (3 words)
39. "Where __ you going?"
40. A drink that comes with its own "bag"
41. Not me
42. Use a place __ instead of a tablecloth
43. Pigs live in a __
44. A wooden pin

Down

1. People read the classified __ to look for jobs
2. A baseball player wears a __ on his head
3. Put mascara on __ lashes
4. Parts of your hands
5. "Did you leave the waiter __ __?"
6. Like a macho male
7. You could eat a spare __ at a barbecue
8. December 24 is Christmas __
9. The letter before "E"
14. A baby likes to sit on Mommy's __
15. "__ whiz!" (Golly)
17. Roads (abbr.)
18. An attorney practices __
19. Monkey
21. Opposite of none
22. A body of water
23. Actor __ Danson
27. The letter after "R"
28. Beeps a horn (rhymes with ROOTS)
29. Ladies use hair __ to keep their hair in place
30. A parent could say, "Do __ — say"
32. A person at a racetrack might make __ __ on a horse
33. __ and cheese sandwich
34. The __ of Good Feeling
35. Place
36. Cheat someone
37. Work in the garden with this tool
38. Camp game, __ of war

Round About

All the answers in this puzzle go round and round the diagram, with the beginning of one word overlapping with some of the letters of the word that comes before it. Begin solving by writing the answer to clue #1 in square #1. Put the answers in the diagram by following the order of the numbers and the heavy dotted lines. When you're done, all the squares will be filled in. Don't get dizzy!

Clues

1. People who aren't in attendance at school are ___.
2. Complete
3. Stay behind
4. Textbook section that lists where subjects are found
5. Additional stuff
6. Speedy
7. A stupid person
8. The capital of Canada
9. Billfold for cash and credit cards
10. Main veggie in salads
11. Grand ___ Station in N.Y.
12. Nearly
13. To play a guitar, you ___ it.
14. The baseball official who yells "Strike!"
15. Take a break and relax
16. Heavy rainfall
17. What a person with a wand practices
18. Symbol on a computer screen

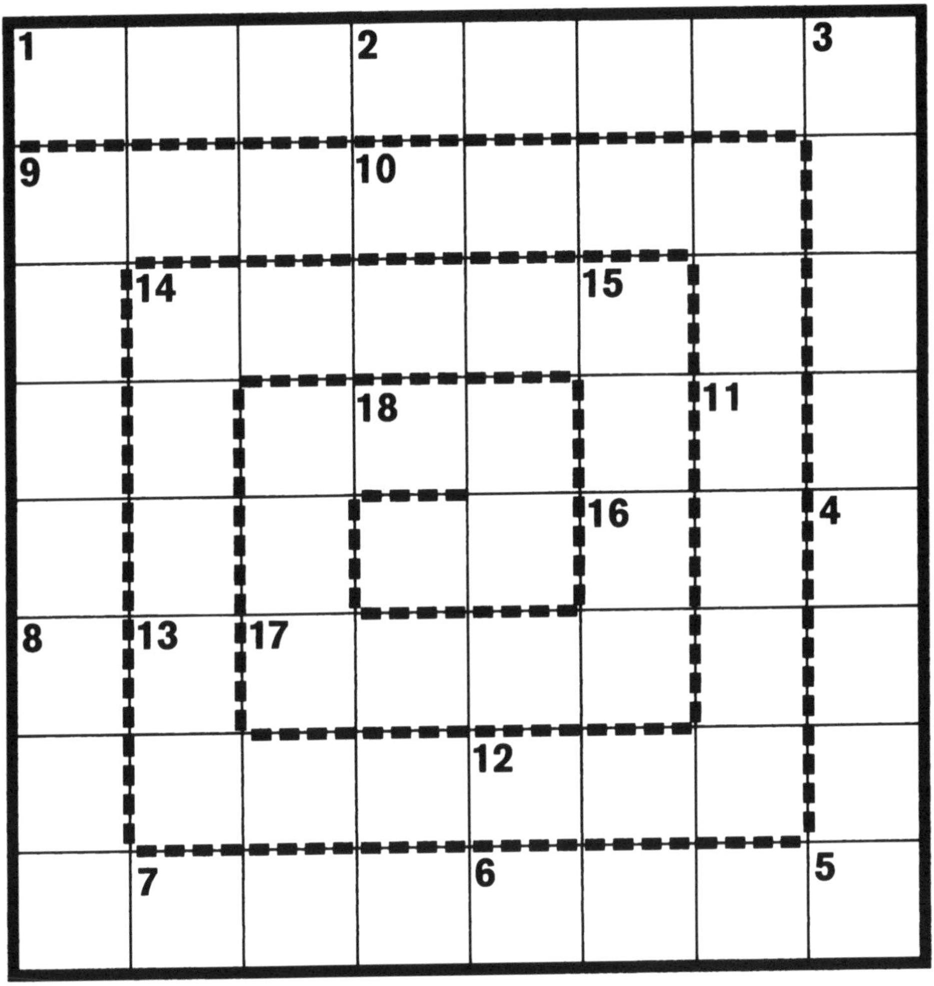
1
2
3
9
10
14
15
18
11
16
4
8
13
17
12
7
6
5

Middles

Fill in the blank space on each line to make a common five-letter word. Be careful! Some blanks can be filled in with a few different letters. Then read DOWN each middle column to find a new word that makes sense. Write the NEW word on the blank space that has the same number as the box. When you're done, read the words from 1 to 18, to find a riddle on this page and its answer on the opposite page. Collapse with laughter when you're done!

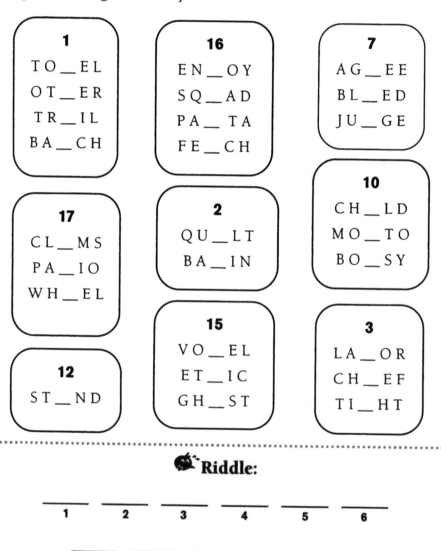

1

TO __ EL
OT __ ER
TR __ IL
BA __ CH

16

EN __ OY
SQ __ AD
PA __ TA
FE __ CH

7

AG __ EE
BL __ ED
JU __ GE

17

CL __ MS
PA __ IO
WH __ EL

2

QU __ LT
BA __ IN

10

CH __ LD
MO __ TO
BO __ SY

12

ST __ ND

15

VO __ EL
ET __ IC
GH __ ST

3

LA __ OR
CH __ EF
TI __ HT

🐷 **Riddle:**

___ ___ ___ ___ ___ ___
1   2   3   4   5   6

___ ___ ___ ___ ___
7   8   9   10   11

11

TA __ FY
SK __ TE
CO __ OA
ST __ EL

9

SP __ ON
FU __ NY

4

BE __ RD
WI __ GS
FU __ GE

18

MU __ IC
CU __ ID
BR __ VE
BE __ IN
AC __ ES
SW __ ET
EX __ RA
AC __ OR
EX __ ST

8

LA __ SO
HA __ PY
AB __ UT
WA __ CH
WA __ TE

6

JE __ EL
QU __ ET
WI __ CH
US __ ER

5

AS __ ES
ST __ GE
SP __ NE
MA __ RY
BU __ ER

14

BR __ VE
PU __ PY
PR __ SS

13

CA __ EL
GR __ ED
PA __ TE
ES __ AY
MA __ BE

🐛 **Riddle Answer:**

___ ___ ___ ___
12 13 14 15

___ ___ ___
16 17 18

State Of Mind

There are no jokes, riddles, or gimmicks here. Just fill in the blanks with the words that answer the clues. Several of the answers are state names.

Across

1. The state next to Kentucky
6. Total
8. Opposite of left
9. Person who takes money for purchases at a store
10. Wrinkle (rhymes with GREASE)
12. A painter puts a canvas on this stand
14. Forty + forty = __
16. Movie director, __ Spielberg
19. A bride walks down the __ at her wedding
21. Playing a character in a movie
24. Pilot of a plane
25. Breakfast roll with a hole in the middle
27. Breakfast food with a yolk
28. The state next to Pennsylvania (2 words)

Down

1. Ripped
2. Complain, complain, complain
3. Additional stuff
4. Sport where you kick the ball
5. Simplest
6. Ocean liners
7. The state next to West Virginia
11. Floor covering
13. A small state next to Virginia
15. The capital city of 28 Across
17. A moving truck
18. Opposite of wide
20. A seat that hangs by a chain and is in a playground
22. Piece of furniture in a dining room
23. Opposite of work
26. Fuel for a car

Actually, there could be a real corny joke here. It's part of an old song.

What did _____?
She wore a brand ___ _____.

Fill in the first blank with the answer to 13 down and the second blank with the answer to 28 across.

Answers

On The Road

Answer: Hop in

Picture Crossword

Answer: Noise

Very Fishy

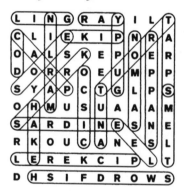

Answer: I'll see you around

Getting There

Answer: Go away!

Mouse Trap

Answer: A Sir Kit (a circuit)

Fractured English

1. Rector
2. Receipt
3. Antidotes
4. Devotes
5. Geyser
6. Insulate
7. Order
8. Symbol
9. Stuff
10. Illegal
11. Fleece
12. Coax
13. Canoe
14. Praise

Weighting Room

Answer: On a diet

Don't Eat Your Veggies

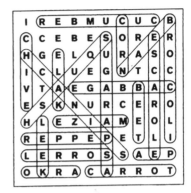

Answer: Iceberg lettuce

Cross Offs

These words are crossed off:
History, Math, Spelling
Clinton, Bush, Kennedy, Truman, Reagan
Honda, Toyota, Volkswagen
Lips, Eyes, Chin
Oatmeal, Applesauce, Soup, Pudding
Acre, Care, Race
Nancy, Mary
Lake, River, Pond
Stallion, Pony, Mare

Leftover words:
Whey gravel on hunches.
Answer:
They travel in bunches.

Staying Connected

Answer: On the web

3-Letter Pieces

Answers:
1. Unique
2. Around
3. Babies
4. Rescue
5. Broken
6. Alaska
7. Square
8. Brunch
9. Monday

Riddle answer: Quicksand

Missing In Action

Answer: The hole works

Go With The Flow

Answer: A car pool

More Missing In Action

Answer: On the outside

Arrow Words #1

Baked Goodies

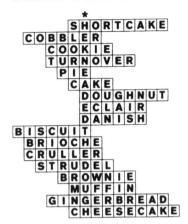

Answer: He kneaded the dough

Just Joking #1

PORCUPINE
HAMSTER
ANTELOPE
HYENA
BURRO

CHEETAH
SQUIRREL
LLAMA

CHIPMUNK
PANTHER

Answer: Cheer him up

Family Byes

Answer: Bison (Bye, son)

Camping Out

Answer: Pup tents

It's A Crime

1. Powerpuff Girls
2. Janet Jackson
3. Al Gore
4. Aaron Carter
5. Mickey Mouse
6. Tori Spelling
7. Backstreet Boys
8. Bill Gates
9. Justin Timberlake
10. Mia Hamm
11. Bugs Bunny
12. Drew Barrymore
13. Scott Foley
14. Tony Hawk
15. Lassie

Daffynition

Answer: Dieting

Find The Riddle

Answers:

Wet	Raw
Rome	Hose
White	Feed
Front	Pry
Key	Charm

Riddle: Why were the workers fired from the tea company?

Up In The Air

Answer: Umbrellas

This Is A Frame-up!

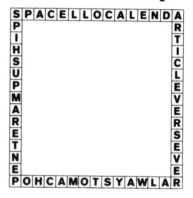

Oh My!

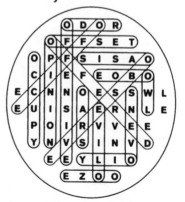

Answer: Eleven
(T-H-E A-L-P-H-A-B-E-T)

Pop Rock

Answer: Cool Music

Crowd Control

House Business?

Answer: Address (a dress)

Computer Confusion

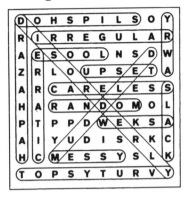

Answer: On sloppy disks

Five 5x5's

Animals	Fruits
1. Horse	1. Berry
2. Panda	2. Apple
3. Camel	3. Peach
4. Tiger	4. Grape
5. Zebra	5. Lemon

Flowers	Instruments
1. Daisy	1. Flute
2. Lilac	2. Piano
3. Pansy	3. Banjo
4. Tulip	4. Organ
5. Poppy	5. Cello

Foreign Countries
1. Spain
2. Italy
3. Egypt
4. China
5. Japan

Night Mare?

Answer: A horse

Piece Of The Pie

Answer: It gets cold

Weather Report

Answer: Poodles

Hue Said It

Answer: Poodles

First/Last

```
      *
F L E A
      H E A R
I D E A
      M I L E
S C A B
      U S E S
R E A L
      A P E S
B A R N
      C O A T
C A P E
```

Answer: A hambulance

Game Plan

Answer Words:

Tennis	Two	Driver
Shop	Old	Rob
Poor	Desk	Buzz
Rich	Kids	Zinc
Hole	Saw	Comic
Elbow	Who	Court
Wet	Odd	

Arrow Words #2

Just Joking #2

*

JUPITER

NEPTUNE

SATURN

EARTH

VENUS

MERCURY

PLUTO

SATELLITE

MARS

URANUS

STAR

GALAXY

SUN

ASTEROID

METEOR

MOON

Answer: In the molar system

Hidden Birds

Double Cross (Word)

Round About

Answer Words:

1. Absent	7. Idiot	13. Strum
2. Entire	8. Ottawa	14. Umpire
3. Remain	9. Wallet	15. Rest
4. Index	10. Lettuce	16. Storm
5. Extra	11. Central	17. Magic
6. Rapid	12. Almost	18. Icon

State Of Mind

Answer: What did Delaware?
She wore a brand New Jersey.

Middles

1.	2.	3.	4.	5.	6.
TOWEL	QUILT	LABOR	BEARD	ASHES	JEWEL
OTHER	BASIN	CHIEF	WINGS	STAGE	QUIET
TRAIL		TIGHT	FUDGE	SPINE	WITCH
BATCH				MARRY	USHER
				BUYER	

7.	8.	9.	10.	11.	12.
AGREE	LASSO	SPOON	CHILD	TAFFY	STAND
BLEED	HAPPY	FUNNY	MOTTO	SKATE	
JUDGE	ABOUT		BOSSY	COCOA	
	WATCH			STEEL	
	WASTE				

13.	14.	15.	16.	17.	18.
CAMEL	BRAVE	VOWEL	ENJOY	CLAMS	MUSIC
GREED	PUPPY	ETHIC	SQUAD	PATIO	CUPID
PASTE	PRESS	GHOST	PASTA	WHEEL	BRAVE
ESSAY			FETCH		BEGIN
MAYBE					ACHES
					SWEET
					EXTRA
					ACTOR
					EXIST

Answer: What is big and hairy with red spots on its face?
A messy ape who just ate spaghetti.